SAM STRICKLAND

# IS LEADERSHIP A RACE?

Orders: please contact Hachette UK Distribution, Hely Hutchinson Centre, Milton Road, Didcot, Oxfordshire, OX11 7HH. Telephone: +44 (0)1235 827827. Email education@hachette.co.uk. Lines are open from 9 a.m. to 5 p.m., Monday to Friday.

ISBN: 9781036006464

© Sam Strickland 2024

First published in 2024 by
John Catt from Hodder Education,
An Hachette UK Company
15 Riduna Park, Station Road,
Melton, Woodbridge IP12 1QT
Telephone: +44 (0)1394 389850
www.johncatt.com

MIX
Paper | Supporting
responsible forestry
FSC™ C104740

*To my family and friends,*
*thank you for your constant support.*

*'You can please some of the people all of the time,*
*you can please all of the people some of the time,*
*but you can't please all of the people all of the time.'*

JOHN LYDGATE

# CONTENTS

# INTRODUCTION:
# THINGS CHANGE

Over time, some things change and other things do not. Prior to the pandemic, some people said that school improvement could be done at a fast pace, almost like a race. Perhaps in some cases this was so, but this type of thinking came about in the early to mid-2000s. It was built on the premise of 'Super Heads' who could lead from the front and transform a school's fortunes in 12 to 18 months. The idea was that this approach was based upon the personality, dynamism and charisma of one key person: namely the 'Super Head'. In reality, this was a flawed model because the changes brought about were not deeply embedded; they were superficial and often fell apart once the Super Head moved on to pastures new. Whilst a school can perhaps be transformed in a relatively short period of time, it takes time to truly embed school improvement. Leadership, in my humble view, is anything but a race.

The Gabarro model of leadership (and therefore school change) is based around the following time frames:

**Stage 1:** This relates to the first six months in post and is the time a new leader sets out their stall. They lay out their vision, what they will bring to the table and what they expect from everyone.

**Stage 2:** This occurs in the second half of the first full year in post, where a leader immerses themselves in the school. They are known to all key stakeholders and people are clear who that leader is and what they are about.

**Stage 3:** This nine-month window is where a leader reshapes things. They may be addressing the model of behaviour or the curriculum, or indeed both. They may be redesigning and redrafting other core areas of the school.

**Stage 4:** This is a period of consolidation, where ideally school improvement and school change slow down and staff are given a chance to embed all of the key changes to date in their day-to-day practice.

**Stage 5:** This takes the new leader into the final phase of their first three years in post. During this phase the leader will reflect on the changes made to date, seeking feedback from key stakeholders and refining approaches accordingly.

**Stage 6:** Following the first three years in post, a leader may well seek to change or reset the pathway of improvement that is in place and recalibrate the culture. However, this can be quite a dangerous phase of school improvement and often stakeholders may be less receptive to new changes.

The overall model proposed by Gabarro looks as follows:

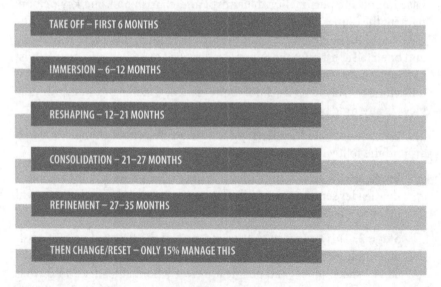

TAKE OFF – FIRST 6 MONTHS

IMMERSION – 6–12 MONTHS

RESHAPING – 12–21 MONTHS

CONSOLIDATION – 21–27 MONTHS

REFINEMENT – 27–35 MONTHS

THEN CHANGE/RESET – ONLY 15% MANAGE THIS

The reality is that school improvement never really transitions smoothly and seamlessly from step A to step B to step C. It can often be messy, challenging and difficult. Invariably there are external factors that can get in the way of the best laid plans. Even the most carefully laid out strategy needs to be underpinned by pragmatism. With the onset of a pandemic, which very few could have foreseen, many school improvement journeys have been derailed and have needed recalibration.

Michael Keaton, playing the iconic superhero Batman, once famously said, 'Things change.' Over the course of the last few years, leadership and school improvement have changed massively. For those who have never sat in the chair, it is hard to comprehend what the role actually entails. Even as a vice principal, I would argue that my understanding of the role was modest at best. During the autumn of 2019 I felt I was in my groove, that I fully understood the role and that I was really hitting my stride. Then, come March 2020, well – things changed.

Those who have studied history and the works of Arthur Marwick will know that war, total war, brings about huge psychological, economic and social change. Simultaneously, institutions are tested. The pandemic essentially replicated the same feel and mindset as a total war. It has involved all, it has changed hearts and minds, it has altered how we view the world and it has brought about huge change. It has also tested many of us without mercy.

Leadership and headship are incredible jobs. I love education. I love teaching. I have the same fire in my belly now as I did when I first became a principal. However, for many leaders and heads, the pandemic caused burnout. Exhaustion, resentment and at worst anger were evident amongst some heads. School leaders were entrusted to serve as a focal point for their communities during the height of the pandemic, free from the pressures of the accountability framework of Ofsted and league tables. They were expected to change – with no notice and with no real training – not just how schools operated and functioned, but education as a whole. Then, with almost no notice again, school leaders have had to revert back to a 'business as usual, accountability is back, nothing to see here' approach. In reality, nothing is now 'normal' compared to how we knew it back in 2019. My observation, rather than opinion, is that the recent anti-Ofsted response is evidence of a profession oozing with a passion and desire for positive and healthy accountability.

However we seek to strip it, heads and leaders are more accountable than ever, yet face extenuating external factors that are actually beyond their control and sphere of influence.

First and foremost, recruitment has changed. One only has to look at the ITT entry figures to see that a huge recruitment issue is not just brewing – it's already here. The reality is that people are seeking either better paid jobs, flexible working or the ability to work from home. Some will argue that it is for school leaders to sell the profession to the public, but there comes a tipping point where infectious enthusiasm becomes delusional and out of touch. Even an increased starting salary of £30,000 per year will not resolve the crisis we face. With league tables back in full flow, the scrutiny of exam results will increase once more. Yes, that is part of the job, but that pressure intensifies if you have a maths department of non-specialists, you haven't got one qualified physics teacher and you have kept your head in the sand over the EBacc because you can't find a linguist for all the tea in China. This becomes a leadership team's problem, for which they are accountable. And whilst the new chain of supply into the profession is beginning to dry up, we see experienced and seasoned teachers and leaders leaving the profession too. Who will replace them? Who will fill the experience vacuum that they will leave behind? What impact will this have on school improvement trajectories?

The pandemic has fundamentally changed how people see work: how they view their work–life balance, their sense of what they are worth financially and how much work they are prepared to do. Historically, during times of economic crisis, teaching has seen an increase in the number of people joining the profession. But things have changed, and irrespective of the current economic uncertainty, people are not gravitating towards education. How I wish it would change, and change fast, for the better.

The pressures on school communities have also increased. Behavioural drift has become a significant issue in many schools, with pupils becoming more challenging, refusing to adhere to rules, sanctions or support. The profession has seen varying crazes inspired by social media. Most notably, we have seen students staging demonstrations, vaping in toilets and taking pictures/films of staff and posting them online. This is to name but a few of the issues that are now prevalent. The situation is compounded by local media outlets jumping to shame schools when a singular parent writes to them to complain about the 'overly stringent' rules school X promotes. School leaders have also seen groups of parents turn to protests, with some high-profile cases of such 'pressure groups' appearing in the national press. This adds yet another layer of pressure to leaders, who are forever anxious about where the boundary of the parent–school social contract lies, and there is a constant fear of 'will this trigger an Ofsted inspection?' The unintended consequence of parents barraging schools and challenging their rules and policies is twofold: one, behaviour will worsen as children will feel legitimised to behave badly as their parents do not like the rules; and two, recruitment will worsen as people will look at teaching as a job that carries little societal respect.

Attendance, safeguarding and mental health present a trio of challenges that I have never seen, to this magnitude, in my career. National attendance data is beyond alarming. Whilst attendance figures may mirror those of the early 2000s, I truly believe it will take even longer now than it did back then to remedy this situation. This presents a huge challenge for heads. How do you support children to catch up on their learning when they are not at school and refusing to engage?

I am yet to speak to a school leader who is not equally alarmed by the growing number of mental health issues that we now see in schools, which directly link to and/or stem from safeguarding issues. Regardless of how anyone wants to strip it, there simply isn't sufficient funding in place for schools to address all the issues that they face, yet leaders continue to feel hugely accountable. The lack of external services, support and alternate provision compounds this further. So, what is the solution? Surely sufficient funding to remedy the crisis schools are facing or a full recalibration of what role schools and education actually play is needed. At present, schools are the focal point for the communities that they serve. There are also many factors outside of school that impact what happens within them, including the economic crisis, forcing parents to choose between heating and food. Families struggle to ensure children are adequately clothed and economically supported so that they can come to school worry free. Again, schools have assumed a role here too.

Then there is the small matter of catch-up. Sir Kevan Collins was clear that education needed billions of pounds invested into it if schools were going to adequately support children to catch up on lost learning. The amount invested thus far is a fraction of the amount that he specified was needed. Children have arguably fallen behind (granted, not all children) academically, socially and developmentally. But the notion of longer school days, external tutors, shortening holidays, etc., adds another layer of pressure on the laps of leaders. The one key element forgotten in the catch-up narrative is children and how they learn. They are not Johnny 5 from *Short Circuit*, a robot capable of inputting information at high speed. They are children who get tired, who can only absorb, learn and retain so much. I do think the pandemic presented us with a number of opportunities to creatively rethink elements of education, which are now lost.

Moving forwards, school leaders are faced with huge uncertainty. Leaders are almost in no man's land at present and are basing decision making on best bets, speculation and doubt. The overall challenges facing schools could be represented as follows:

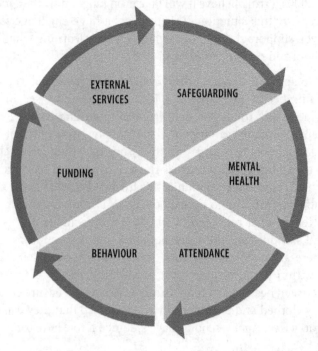

The latest NEU findings highlight that supporting staff wellbeing and mental health, dealing with safeguarding and supporting pupil welfare are significant issues that face leaders. They also state that 80% of leaders think their workload is unacceptable and 83% of leaders cannot find the time to be strategic. NEU findings also state that leaders work long hours every week – longer than pre-pandemic levels. There is also a clear difference between primary leaders, who are having to focus on budget management more and more, and secondary leaders, who are saddled with recruitment and retention issues coupled with poor pupil behaviour and attendance. The overall picture could be deemed bleak.

However, there are three things that remain true. Firstly, since schools have fully returned following the pandemic, the goalpost has shifted. Secondly, we can derive huge satisfaction from working with children and our colleagues, and what we do really does make a difference. Finally, it remains that great schools improve the life chances of children. Equally, children do not have the agency to decide upon their education. So, how do we ensure that what we have to offer is the best it can possibly be? This book is going to outline a number of vital areas that underpin school improvement, and cover changes and approaches that can have a positive impact on the lives of children.

Before you immerse yourself in this book, and I really hope that you do, it is worth considering the following questions:

1. What is it like to be educated and/or work in your school?

2. What impact does your school have on your community?

3. What role have you played to ensure that the quality of education in your school is better now than when you first joined?

I hope that this book supports you to engage in deeply rooted, positive and transformational change that is long lasting and sustained within your school community.

# CHAPTER 1:
# DO YOU KNOW WHO YOU ARE?

*'Knowing yourself is the beginning of all wisdom.'*
ARISTOTLE

This chapter will focus on two important elements:

1. What is leading?
2. Knowing yourself before you can lead others.

However we strip it, leading is hard. You are always going to be faced with problematic situations that, deep down, you would probably wish you did not have to respond to. Nothing is ever fixed. As cited in the introduction, school improvement is not a seamless journey. At some stage you will, invariably, have to make a decision (or set of decisions) that is not popular. This does not mean you should not operate in a manner that is kind, decent and humble.

Before you climb the greasy pole of educational leadership and move up the hierarchy, I would like to pose a few questions for you to reflect upon, as follows:

1. Why do you want to be a leader?
2. Does leadership seem to be the next natural step in your career?
3. Do you simply want to earn more money?
4. Are you seeking some form of assumed position of power?
5. Do you want to make a fundamentally positive difference?

Question five is critical. Leadership should be about making a fundamentally positive difference to others. It should be about wanting to lead a community. Your focus and drive should be about supporting the life chances of children and the professional development of other teachers. All too often I see people who engage in a high-speed race to the top but ultimately lack the depth of experience required for senior leadership. Leadership really does not need to be a race. Once you move up the ladder you only truly know what you know, and if you lack the necessary touchstones that come from lived experience, you are going to be found wanting. Whilst I fully appreciate the benefits that research brings, you equally cannot research your way out of a major safeguarding crisis or an Ofsted inspection that has not gone quite as you had hoped.

As a leader, you want to hit the sweet spot where high performance becomes a habit – as natural as brushing your teeth. If you find that magical pot of gold at the end of the rainbow, then bottle up the secret and sell it, as you will become a millionaire! The reality is that no leader is the finished product, and setting a high bar of expectation for yourself, your team and your community is key to your success. The work of being a leader, though, is never truly done. As businessman and philanthropist Steve Morgan famously said, 'Thou shalt work like hell.' To be successful in leadership you have to be prepared to put in the hard yards.

As a leader, you are now part of the mothership (the school). When people talk about the school, the truth is they are talking about you. There is a clear difference between being a middle leader and a senior leader. Your relationship with (and how you are viewed by) the staff transitions when you become senior leader, whether you like it or not. The same can be said for how pupils and parents will view you too. As a leader, you will be seen as part of the senior leadership team, part of the established (or yet to be cemented) order. People will, like it or not, expect you to have all of the answers. You cannot repeatedly fudge this when asked. Yes, you can say to staff 'I will come back to you on this', but you cannot make that approach a permanent habit or staff will quickly lose faith in you and find it disconcerting. As a new leader, you will question your own agency and at times feel like a brand-new teacher. You will inevitably look at other leaders and question how they make everything look so easy. The swan-like grace that appears to be employed by others is something that newer and less experienced leaders often look upon with envy. Trust me – irrespective of your experience and expertise, you never truly feel the finished article.

Within the context of any given leadership team, the head should really serve as the backstop. This is the person that you should be able to go to for advice and guidance. They should support you and allow you to perform your job effectively. More domineering, controlling heads need to be careful with the balance of autonomy versus control that they employ, so as not to become overly suffocating.

Lambert stated that 'the function of leadership must be to engage people in the processes that create conditions for learning and form common ground about teaching and learning'.[1] Broadly, I agree with this statement. The role of leaders is to generate a school culture, climate and ethos where teachers can teach disruption free and pupils can learn. Irrespective of educational philosophy and ideological views, I imagine there would be near unanimity over this ideal. I believe that this is an ideal, as disruption-free teaching is not commonplace in so many schools.

With all of this in mind, it is important to consider how you fit into the type of school that you are working in. It is why context is king. Do you work in a school that is engaging in a seismic transformation as the school is in a mess? Do you work in a school that serves as an umbrella for staff, that shields them from endless nonsense and takes the view that classrooms are where the magic happens? Are you part of a team that serves as a vanguard for a school's culture, where the culture is deeply embedded and has been in place for a long time? Are middle leaders left to serve as the masters of their own fiefdoms and generate their own localised cultures? Is the school built around a totally devolved approach and staff are expected to figure it all out for themselves? Or are you in a school where the culture runs like a rod of iron and everything is explicitly spelled out? You may well be in a school where it is a hybrid of these types. There are two key considerations:

1. All roads lead to Rome. In the case of school culture, they all lead to the head. The head is responsible for the day-to-day culture, climate and ethos of the school.

---

1 Lambert, L. (2002) 'Toward a deepened theory of constructivist leadership.' In: *The Constructivist Leader*, Lambert, L. et al., pp. 34–62.

2. Where do you fit into the school's culture, assuming you are a leader and not the head?

It is therefore really important, before you even attempt to set the tone, that you consider yourself as a leader. There are a number of critical questions that I am going to pose to you, and I really recommend taking the time to reflect upon each of these for yourself.

- What sort of leader are you?
- What sort of leader do you want to be?
- How true to yourself are you?
- What do you believe in?
- What do you stand for?
- What drives you?
- What is your moral purpose?
- What are your values?
- What are your areas of strength and, as much as you may not like it, your weaknesses?
- How do you respond to intense pressure and pressured situations where you have to make high-speed decisions?
- Where professionally do you want to be and what is your ideal self?

If you have not considered these questions and written down responses to truly reflect upon yourself as a leader, then I wholeheartedly recommend that you do. You have to know yourself before you lead others. Leading is about how you work with others – how you inspire other people to do their jobs. It is about being human, about employing your emotional intelligence, about providing people with clarity and certainty. None of this can be done if you do not understand yourself first and foremost. You simply cannot lead other people if you do not know yourself.

Boyatzis talks about the ideal self. Through the Boyatzis model, which can be quite a complex leadership tool to navigate, potential leaders (and existing ones) are, broadly speaking, encouraged to think about who they are at this current point in time, what their strengths and areas for development are, and their ideal self (who do I want to be?). The ideal-self model can be simplified to look as follows:

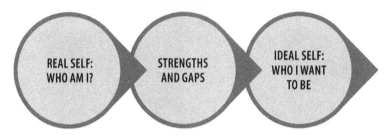

Take the time to create your own ideal-self model, write it down, display it somewhere or put it away in an envelope, and come back to it in six to 12 months' time and see where you are in your journey to becoming your ideal self.

Once you have a handle on who you are, you then need to consider the school you work for. It is a common misconception that all schools have the same mission. Maybe the overarching theme of 'we are here to educate children' is common, but every school has its own 'way', approach, methodology, views on curriculum and behaviour, approaches to CPD, mission statement, vision and values. A critical question to ask yourself is 'am I mission aligned?' In other words, do you fundamentally believe in what your particular school stands for and are you prepared to defend it to the world?

Once you know you are mission aligned, you then need to consider that being a leader really is a role based on enabling. You will, through your work, need to enable the following, which I will be discussing throughout this book:

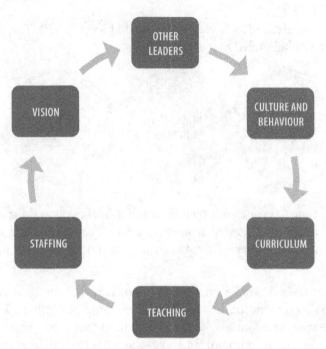

I would also argue that there are some major misconceptions and issues within leadership that we all need to be aware of before we embark on laying the foundations of our school improvement ambitions, as follows:

1. School transformation should operate at high speed.

2. You must change your leadership style to suit the situation that presents itself to you.

3. You must operate as an island and leadership is about doing, doing, doing.

4. Being outwardly, visibly busy and telling everyone you are busy makes you effective.

5. Constant changes are a positive and what people crave and need.

6. Working long hours relentlessly is key.

Once you are confident and comfortable in your own skin (and believe me, to serve as leader you really do need to be), you should really reflect on four core areas that will make you *you*, your team what it is and your school what it outwardly conveys itself to be. Namely:

**A: You**
We have already covered that knowing yourself is crucial. But your self-awareness, self-control, self-conduct, self-care and self-esteem are key.

**B: Your educational philosophy**
This is the fundamental belief set that underpins your actions as a leader.

**C: Your story and your school's story**
Arguably, the school's story carries greater weight and relevancy. This is your narration of what your school is about. The more compelling this is, the more likely it is that people will come with you.

**D: The team**
Who are the people that work with and/or for you? What makes them tick? What are their values, beliefs and expertise levels? It is crucial to know this if you are to move forwards.

If I take this a little deeper – and it is why context is absolutely crucial – as a leader, you are pulling together a complex and interconnected community of contextual factors. Some of these may complement one another, some may actually be competing and at odds with each other. You are trying to strike a balance between the following:

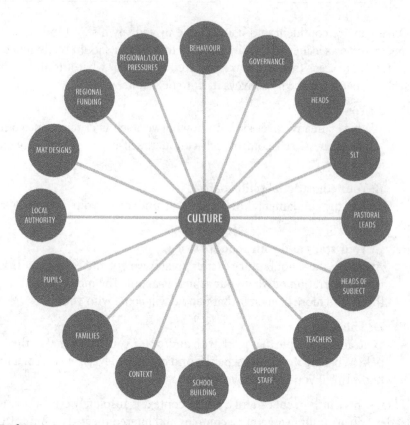

Before you even consider how you want your school to look or to be, what it stands for, and what its vision, values and ethos are, you must consider all of these variables in what I call 'the interconnected school'. No two schools are the same. A giant all-through school of 2000 pupils is not the same as a free school of 500 pupils. An independent school is not the same as an inner-city mixed comprehensive. A one-form entry infant school is not the same as a three-form entry primary. And so on.

As I bring chapter one to a close, I hope I have provoked you to think deeply about who you are, the type of leader you aspire to be and the importance of your school's culture. You cannot simply set about leading on high-speed school improvement without, at the very least, an appreciation of these factors. I would like to end this chapter with six quotes, and all I ask is for you to reflect on them and consider whether they resonate with you. If they do, why? What do they mean both to you and for you?

**QUOTE 1**

*'If your actions inspire others to dream more, learn more, do more and become more, you are a leader.'*

JOHN QUINCY ADAMS

**QUOTE 2**

*'Leaders must be tough enough to fight, tender enough to cry, human enough to make mistakes, humble enough to admit them, strong enough to absorb the pain, and resilient enough to bounce back and keep on moving.'*

JESSE JACKSON

**QUOTE 3**

*'The very essence of leadership is that you have to have vision. You can't blow an uncertain trumpet.'*

THEODORE HESBURGH

**QUOTE 4**

*'Leadership is the capacity to translate vision into reality.'*

WARREN G BENNIS

**QUOTE 5**

*'A leader takes people where they want to go. A great leader takes people where they don't necessarily want to go, but ought to be.'*

ROSALYNN CARTER

**QUOTE 6**

*'A leader is best when people barely know that he exists, not so good when people obey and acclaim him, worst when they despise him. Fail to honor people, they fail to honor you. But of a good leader, who talks little, when his work is done, his aims fulfilled, they will all say, "We did this ourselves."'*

LAO TZU

Now would be a good time to write down five key takeaways that you will action on the basis of what you have read in chapter one. (There is extra space for notes at the back of the book.)

**Considerations:**

**1**

**2**

**3**

**4**

**5**

CHAPTER 2:

# BE TRUE TO WHO YOU ARE

*'The truth will set you free. But not until it is finished with you.'*
DAVID FOSTER WALLACE

---

This chapter will focus on three important elements:

1. The role leadership styles can/cannot play
2. Dealing with crises
3. Being true to who you are.

---

In chapter one we considered what leading is and the importance of knowing yourself. This chapter will focus on being true to yourself, adopting your own leadership persona and how you maintain this in times of absolute crisis.

As the old saying goes, first impressions count. My starting point with you as a leader, and indeed leadership as a whole, is that people will judge you. Everyone will judge you. From the car you drive, to the clothes you wear, to the way you conduct yourself, to how you treat people and to your every message, be it via email, in person or in a wider public forum, people will judge you. Without doubt on a Friday night, as some staff members socialise, parents send messages in WhatsApp groups and pupils post on social media channels, someone somewhere will be talking about you. They will give an opinion on your leadership and what you bring to the table. As a leader, if you truly want to be effective and don't want to be suffocated, you need to block this out. This is essentially white noise and something of a trap. That is not to say that we should be tone deaf to what our communities are telling us, but that feedback needs to come via the right channel. You should not allow tittle-tattle to penetrate your mind. If you allow it to, it will consume you. You will quickly develop imposter syndrome, which will make you think that you cannot do the job you have been appointed to perform and that maybe being a leader was and is a mistake. You need to somehow accept that you will always, irrespective of any decision you make, have a critic. It is what I call Judge Dredd syndrome. In short, you will be judged **but** do not dread it.

Another key element of leadership is what people do and do not know about you. Some leaders like to be guarded about how much they share with staff, whereas other leaders arguably overshare. Getting the balance right can be quite tricky. There is a need to demonstrate to staff that you are human, that you care, that you are bothered and that, just like them, you have feelings. However, how much you want to share can vary greatly from person to person, leader to leader. The Johari Window is a useful tool to refer to here. This tool encourages you to consider four key areas, namely your open/free area, your hidden area, your unknown area and your blind area. Each of these four areas can be defined as follows:

1.  The open/free area refers to what you know and what others also know about you. Simply put, this is the information that you freely share with other people. This could be your role, your title and a few personal details about yourself.

2.  The unknown area is what is unknown to both yourself and others. They can be feelings, behaviours or attitudes that can be quite close to the surface. This area tends to become more obvious as you work more readily with other people over time.

3.  The blind area is what you do not know about yourself but what other people seem to know about you.

4.  The hidden area is what you know about yourself that others do not know. This tends to be personal or private information about yourself that you would prefer not to share.

The Johari Window for a new leader broadly looks as follows:

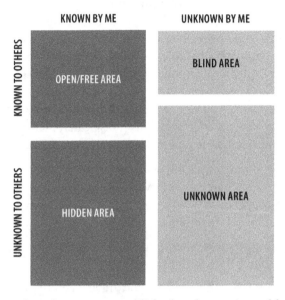

The Johari Window for a more established and experienced leader tends to look as follows:

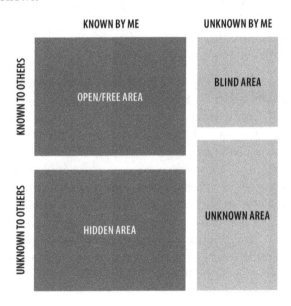

It's worth taking 10 minutes to consider this for yourself and sketching out how your own Johari Window looks. I would then recommend sharing this with a few close colleagues and gauging their thoughts and responses. This could be really telling and may lead you to rethink the way in which you approach your role at school. Given the ideas I presented in the previous chapter about knowing yourself, it would also be worthwhile marrying up and comparing your personalised Johari Window to your ideal self and where you are currently. All of this work and quiet self-reflection will serve to offer you a clear, or clearer, picture of the type of leader that you are and the type of leader you want to be.

As a leader you will invariably experience an array of mindsets every single week, every single day and even every single hour. No two days are the same. Your eyes become more and more tuned to what is wrong than what is right. You can experience a series of states, including:

- Surfing – this is where you are riding the wave, and everything seems to be going right for you.
- Swimming – this is where you are just coping, and you are only just staying afloat.
- Sinking – this is where things are going wrong, and you cannot keep on top.
- Drowning – this is a critical state where everything appears and feels as though it is going wrong for you.

When you are drowning you are in your most dangerous phase as a leader. This is where you can easily make rushed and very poor decisions, which ultimately will come back to haunt you. When you are in a state of sinking or drowning, you must look to other senior leaders for help, support and counsel. There is also a real danger when you are in this state that you will become something of a Han Solo, seeking to do everything as an island. A similar state is where you feel the need to serve as a superhero. Operating in this state can be highly dangerous. Leaders who do this often generate a sense amongst staff that they, and they alone, can save everyone. It is really important when you are sinking or drowning to quite literally stop! To pause! To think carefully about what you are doing and why. I would recommend writing down 10 core tasks that you need to do (invariably there will be more as leaders are always having to spin multiple and endless plates) and then carefully consider the following:

- Do you personally have to do the task?
- Can you ignore the task?
- Can you delegate the task?
- Does the task add any value?
- Can the task be delayed/postponed to a future point in time?
- Who has asked you to do it and why?

An interesting view on leadership was offered by education consultant John Dunford. He said that 'good leaders do not have a single leadership style. You adapt to suit the situation.'[2] In some regards I can see what the point of this quote is – that you need to respond accordingly to situations and problems as they face you. This brings into play theoretical leadership styles such as being an authoritarian, being dictatorial, being dogged, operating as a devolved leader, being compassionate, being humble, etc. The danger with adapting your leadership style is that you may well end up being at odds with who you actually are. I call this the chameleon effect. If you are forever changing the outward appearance that you adopt to (theoretically) suit the situation that faces you, then you actually run the risk of alienating yourself from other members of staff. People may well question who you actually are and your overall authenticity. At the absolute worst you could knock staff members off their centre of gravity and lead them to really question just how trustworthy you are. My overall advice is to be your own person, to be true to yourself and to never stray from your own moral purpose. People will follow you if you are authentic, honest and lead with integrity. They are far less likely to follow you, truly follow you, if you shoot from the hip, are forever changing your approach and if people do not know how you will react in challenging situations.

As a leader, especially as a head, you will invariably have to deal with some really high-level problems and resolve some serious mistakes. As you read the following situations that could easily face you as a leader, I would like you to consider two things: how would you respond to this situation (what

---

2    https://johndunfordconsulting.wordpress.com/2011/11/01/ten-things-learned-on-my-leadership-journey/

would your solution be?) and how would you genuinely handle yourself outwardly towards your colleagues?

**Situation 1:** Ofsted have called you and they are sat in your school's car park. They will be commencing a no-notice safeguarding inspection in 15 minutes due to serious concerns about your school's safeguarding protocols and processes.

**Situation 2:** You have been in post for four days as the head of a school and you have just received a call from Ofsted that you will face a Section 8 monitoring visit tomorrow.

**Situation 3:** It has started to snow in the middle of the day. The local factories and industrial areas have closed their workplaces due to the snow, and reception is full of parents demanding to take their children home. Most of your staff live remotely from the school in difficult to reach areas when the weather is inclement. The snow is falling at pace as you process what is happening.

**Situation 4:** A pandemic breaks and you have to make decisions quickly, with little notice and little guidance.

**Situation 5:** Your school predictions are significantly off. You thought your school was going to achieve very strong outcomes and the pupils have hugely underperformed in all areas.

**Situation 6:** Your premises manager has just come to notify you that rats have been discovered in the corridors of the school. If you close, you risk huge reputational damage; if you remain open, you risk the safety of staff and pupils.

**Situation 7:** There is a water leak in your school and the only way to contain it is to turn all of the water off, which means that there will be no running water in your school. The earliest someone can come fix it is in 18 hours.

**Situation 8:** You have made a critical and necessary change to an aspect of the behaviour system, but this has resulted in some parents responding negatively. Six parents have clubbed together and have sent formal complaints to the school. They have notified the local press, the local MP, set up a change.org petition and contacted Ofsted.

**Situation 9:** Throughout the course of the morning swathes of pupils have come down with a sickness bug. You have pupils unwell in many areas of the school and there are many pupils vomiting. It is clear that you have a norovirus outbreak on your hands.

Without wishing to sound too alarmist or pessimistic, these are all situations that could face any head or leadership team in any school. How you respond to these crises is key. Equally, mistakes in schools will and do happen. Sometimes a clear, confident and decisive approach to leadership is needed, but this should not be mistaken for changing your persona.

There also needs to be a healthy acceptance that mistakes can and will happen. I call this the 1000 decision-making reality. In the course of any school day, all of us, be it class teachers, middle leaders, senior leaders, heads, executive leaders, etc., will make 1000+ decisions. Most of these are micro decisions. Due to the law of probability, and being a human, you are likely to get at least one of these decisions wrong. You cannot possibly ensure that every single decision you ever make is 100% correct. Mistakes can, do and will happen. How mistakes are viewed, received and responded to is part of your organisation's culture. When a mistake occurs, it is important to consider:

- Will the mistake be held against me?
- Are we able to discuss mistakes as a team?
- Is it safe to take a risk?
- Is it difficult to ask other members of the team for help?
- Am I valued?
- Are my contributions valued?

My view when faced with a problem, mistake or crisis is to create a solution circle, whereby you work as a team to come to a resolution or series of solutions. Within a solution circle, you are essentially working as a team to generate a sense of how you will tackle the problem. One member of the team presents what the problem is and has up to five minutes to outline and detail the problem. As a team you should then take one minute to reflect on what has been said and a further minute to jot down questions and solutions. Then take a further five minutes to ask key questions for clarity. Following the questions, another two minutes should be taken individually to consider solutions and unintended consequences that could stem from those solutions. Then ask each member of the team one at a time (allow five minutes in total for this) to share their solutions to the problem. One member of the team should write these down. Once everyone has spoken, the person scribing should read out the solutions offered and as a team discuss either your outright solution or the relevant number of actions you will take as a team. Then assign who will do what. Once you have agreed on a pathway to resolve your issue, take a further two minutes to consider what the unintended consequences of your actions could be before you press ahead. Visually this approach looks as follows:

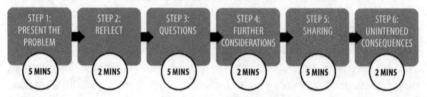

A different approach to resolving a problem could be to adopt the Toyoda method, where as a team you discuss the problem at hand and ask 'why' five times to really try to get to the heart of the problem at hand. Using this approach, you are literally asking:

- Why did this happen?
- Why did this happen?
- Why did this happen?
- Why did this happen?
- Why did this happen?

By asking why each subsequent stage of a problem happened five times, but not in an accusatory manner, you are really trying to get under the skin of why something has gone wrong, and then you can consider what you need to do to resolve it and mitigate against it happening again.

As I bring this chapter to a close, I hope I have made you consider in a little more depth who you are, the role of leadership styles and the importance of being true and honest to who you are, and I hope I have made you think about crisis situations that I hope you never have to face. Queen Elizabeth II said, 'I know of no single formula for success. But over the years I have observed that some attributes of leadership are universal and are often about finding ways to encourage people to combine their efforts, their talents, their insights, their enthusiasm and their inspiration to work together.' This key observation from our recently deceased Queen is incredibly astute and very much in line with my thinking regarding what the role of being a leader in a school actually entails.

My final thought for you, often attributed to Oscar Wilde, is 'be yourself; everyone else is taken'. The very best leadership style you can adopt for yourself is *your* leadership style.

Now would be a good time to write down five key takeaways that you will action for yourself on the basis of what you have read in chapter two.

**Considerations:**

**1**

_____

_____

**2**

_____

_____

**3**

_____

_____

**4**

_____

_____

**5**

_____

_____

# CHAPTER 3:
# RESPECT YOUR CONTEXT – PRIOR PLANNING PREVENTS POOR PERFORMANCE

*'Don't ever make decisions based on fear. Make decisions based on hope and possibility. Make decisions based on what should happen, not what shouldn't.'*

MICHELLE OBAMA

---

This chapter will focus on two important elements:

1. The importance of context
2. Why you need to plan strategically before you execute your actions.

---

As a less experienced senior leader I was, with hindsight, professionally naïve and prone to making mistakes. My view of leadership was that it was all about doing, doing and doing some more. Being seen to be busy, to be active and to make changes was surely what being a leader was all about. I distinctly remember the first time I heard about mission alignment, mission statements, vision statements and values. I thought that this was all absolute nonsense (or slightly stronger words with a similar point). The reality is that the context, mission, vision, values and ethos of an organisation – any organisation – are not just critical to its success but the bedrock upon which everything is built. British Paralympics GB is founded upon a clear vision statement that states: 'Through sport, inspire a better world for disabled people.' The Royal Marines, an elite fighting machine, are built upon the premise of the Commando Spirit. Underpinning this are four core principles, namely courage, determination, unselfishness and cheerfulness. The SAS, in a similar vein, are built upon the principles of:

PLAN        BRIEF        EXECUTE        DEBRIEF

Save the Children is built upon four clear strategic goals, with 'we hold children's rights at the heart of everything we do' serving as their most important goal. One of the most successful English football clubs in the modern era, Manchester City, is built upon the motto 'superbia in proelio', which translates into English as 'pride in battle'. The point is that the mission statement, vision, values and ethos of the school you work at, just like the military or a big and successful organisation or football club, are important. They are part of your school's identity. They allow you to justify the 'why' behind your decision making. They will underpin the morals and reasoning for taking the action(s) that you are likely to take, and as a result they become harder to argue against. My critical piece of advice, though, is if an action or change you are going to bring about falls outside the parameters of your school's ethos, vision and values, then do not do it. You will struggle to win over the hearts and minds of your stakeholders, and whilst people may well go with your change, they won't truly believe in what they are doing. My other piece of advice is to keep the focus of your mission statement, vision and values about people and children. Ultimately, we work in a people-driven sector, and education is all about human interaction. It is not some sterile environment where people are akin to robots.

The context of any school is also critically important. I appreciate I have already stated this, but no two schools are equal. The following (and by no means exhaustive) list contains factors to consider for your school and the strategic direction of travel:

- The geographical positioning of the school
- Employment levels within your locality

- The number of languages spoken by the children and families making up your school community
- The number of children with SEN and the number that hold an EHCP
- The number of pupils who are in receipt of free school meals or Pupil Premium
- What recruitment and retention of staff are like in your geographical area
- The experience profile and level of expertise of the staffing body
- The age profile and level of expertise of leaders within the school
- The training and wider professional development staff have had access to
- Whether your school is a single academy trust, a local authority school or in a multi-academy trust
- The aspirations of the local community
- Safeguarding matters localised to where you are based
- Funding (this is unevenly distributed nationally)
- The behaviour of the pupils
- The existing systems, processes and procedures in place
- The long-standing ethos of the school and how embedded it is
- The curricular philosophy that is in place and how mature and developed the curriculum is
- The policies in place
- The approaches to workload in place
- The size of the school cohort
- The size of the school building, how modern it is and the geography of the building
- The location of the classrooms
- Whether the school is all under one roof or spread across multiple buildings or a split site

- The size of eatery areas, halls, playgrounds and other critical facilities
- Staffing contracts (is there a trust contract in place? Are you regulated by standard teacher terms and conditions? etc.)
- How unionised the staff you work with are and the overall union presence and representation in the school
- The attitude of former leaders to the staff
- The influence and role of governors, trust central teams, etc.
- Trust directions (if you are in a multi-academy trust)
- The external accountability outcomes
- The Ofsted rating of your establishment.

These are but a few of the considerations that you *must* take into account when you consider your school and its direction of travel. Whilst research and evidence-informed approaches are great and absolutely have a place in schools and education, we cannot look at evidence in isolation. It is far more complex and nuanced than simply taking the view that research says X, therefore I must do Y. Schools are hugely complex, fluid and challenging organisations. You must pay respect to your context, even if your contextual setting needs a seismic shake-up.

There are five critical touchstones that you must consider when you are seeking to lead and bring about change, namely:

1. Your context (I appreciate I have laboured this point).

2. You – your expertise, experience and the touchstones you can draw upon are crucial. This is why the first two chapters of the book have focused so much on you as a leader.

3. Research and evidence – whilst not all evidence is equal, it is important to know what is out there, what has been endorsed and what the big best bets are.

4. Key partners – do not operate as an island. Forge links with other schools and educational partners both locally and nationally. The more cross-fertilisation of ideas, advice and guidance you can engage with, the better.

5. Sector-wide guidance – there are individuals out there who have done what you are seeking to do. Many are truly generous with their time and expertise. Pick their brains.

You could pare this back to further simplify your key touchstones to a three-pronged set of factors, as follows:

Jim Collins and Jerry Porras talk about BHAG. In other words, having a Big, Hairy, Audacious Goal. This is a big long-term goal set by leaders. Leaders in essence set a goal, then lay out a series of behaviours that will allow the organisation to achieve said goal. They provide training and support where applicable or necessary, and then leaders trust people to get on with it. Arguably, this is a founding principle upon which the US military is built. So, what does this have to do with the price of fish? In an educational setting, I would argue that the same principle can be applied. Once you have carefully considered your context, be it the school as a whole or an area that you are in charge of, you need to identify what your BHAG is. There needs to be a big, clear goal that you are looking to achieve. This should be underpinned by the school's mission statement. A really big goal may well be something that you are aspiring to become or achieve and, a little like building a cathedral, you may never actually get there. Suddenly this sounds a little aloof or pointless. Why would you have a goal set that you cannot achieve? Well, the rationale is that this becomes something you are striving towards. School improvement is never actually done, and a bit like the Holy Grail, you are continually searching for it. Through the process of working towards your BHAG you will, if you set the tone right, bring people with you. You will galvanise hearts and minds. People will be behind you. In doing this, things will change; they will evolve for the better.

The first task is to identify your BHAG and set a time frame for achieving or working towards this. I would argue that it takes five years to truly work towards something big, and this is why leadership is not a race. It is therefore important to have a five-year plan in place. Each of the five years should have an underpinning one-year plan, with one big, clear focus and no more than three drivers. You could set this out to look as follows:

| Overall BHAG: ................................................................................. | | | | | |
|---|---|---|---|---|---|
| | Year 1 | Year 2 | Year 3 | Year 4 | Year 5 |
| Focus | | | | | |
| Core drivers | 1:<br><br>2:<br><br>3: | | | | |

I am a big believer that key documents should fit on a page. There is no reason why your improvement plan cannot fit on one sheet of paper. It does not have to be a document that weighs a ton and is as thick as a brick. If you want to bring people with you, then remember that people believe in leaders who talk to them, listen, show they care and lead by example. They don't tend to listen and truly follow people who produce nice PowerPoint slides and endless lengthy documents that they themselves, if we are truly honest, do not have the time to read.

Now would be a good time for you to pause and think carefully about the following seven questions – the magnificent seven:

1.  What does your contextual setting tell you about your school?
2.  What one big thing needs changing that would make the biggest difference to your establishment?
3.  What is your BHAG?
4.  What will you remove to afford people the time to prioritise your BHAG?
5.  What is getting in the way of your BHAG? Is it genuinely necessary or just white noise?
6.  Does your BHAG explicitly, clearly and directly link to your mission statement, vision and values as an organisation?
7.  Can you explain your BHAG and how to achieve it in under 10 minutes? If not, perhaps what you are asking is too complicated.

Once you have addressed these questions, which are crucial to the success of your plan, it is then important to think hard about the behaviours that you want to see exhibited to achieve this goal. I would urge you to map the core behaviours that you want against your school values and then map these against what you want staff and pupils to demonstrate. You could set this out as follows:

| Values | Behaviours | Teacher | Pupil |
|---|---|---|---|
| 1: | | | |
| 2: | | | |
| 3: | | | |

You then need to consider how you will articulate the plan and the behaviours to your stakeholders. You should carefully consider where and when you will train them, how frequently and routinely you will train them, how to bring them with you and, crucially, when and how to evaluate your actions and their relative successes.

A crucial piece of advice regarding decision making is, where possible, to sleep on a decision. Ensure that you have taken the time to reflect on what you are doing, why you are doing it, how you will do it and whether there are lessons that can be learnt from other organisations. The temptation in leadership is to effect change at speed and to keep on effecting change because (and this was a flaw of my younger and more naïve self) the view is that leadership is all about doing, doing and doing some more. Rushing is your biggest threat and it could be your biggest Achilles heel. Taking your time is not a weakness; it is a strength. Sitting still and waiting intelligently are difficult and challenging leadership behaviours to carry out, **but** they are often vital. It is also important to remember that in order to bring people with you they will also need time and space to consider and understand what you want from them. Therefore, making an announcement on a Friday afternoon briefing that needs to come into effect as of Monday or holding a key piece of training on an INSET day in September that needs to come into play the next day is, most likely, going to fall flat on its face at best and, at worst, push an entire body of people away from you. However we strip it, prior planning prevents poor performance. If I was in the military, then there would be a sixth p, but I will leave that to your imagination.

Now would be a good time to write down five key takeaways that you will action for yourself on the basis of what you have read in chapter three:

**Considerations:**

**1**

**2**

**3**

**4**

**5**

# CHAPTER 4:
# LEADERSHIP IS ALL ABOUT PEOPLE

*'Coming together is a beginning. Staying together is progress. Working together is success.'*
HENRY FORD

> This chapter will focus on three important elements:
> 1. The importance of people to schools
> 2. Why taking your time with people is crucial
> 3. The importance and power of building teams.

So far, this book has focused on what leadership is, which is crucial to your overall understanding of what being a leader is. Time has been taken to consider yourself, because without knowing who you are you simply cannot lead others. Crucially this book has also asked you to carefully consider the contextual setting you find yourself in and to think hard about how you formulate your game plan to drive the changes you want to see. I have a lot of admiration for the work of Stephen R. Covey. He created Covey's devices and, simplistically put, he identified four core devices for school improvement, namely:

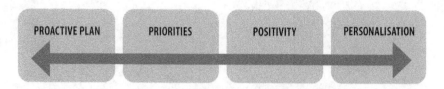

In the previous chapter, we examined the importance of having a proactive plan and the underpinning core priorities to make this happen. Throughout this book I would argue that positivity has been covered, but this should be a mainstay of your overall demeanour and approach. I do not mean manufactured or false positivity but genuine enthusiasm for the work that you are carrying out. If, as a leader, you are not positive about what you are doing and do not demonstrate this positivity, then I would argue you do not truly believe in what you are doing, or you are always looking for excuses for why something won't work. Your mindset as a leader is really important. However, this chapter is going to focus on the personalisation aspect of Covey's devices, and within that, one of the most important factors and variables that you will have to work with: people.

Much is made of education being like a business; of our need to cut our cloth accordingly with school budgets, to secure positive external gradings and to climb the league tables. I do not doubt their importance to the success of any given institution and how any given school is viewed by its community. However, what is often forgotten is that education is a people-based sector. In leading a school, you are leading people, you are working with other leaders and you are in charge of a staffing body and a pupil population. You are also going to have to interact with governors and parents, and potentially local councillors, MPs and the local media. The point is everything comes back to one thing: people. Without other people on your side, without people working with and for you and believing in what you are doing, you are more than likely destined to fail. You can have the most evidence-informed, well-read and well-thought-through game plan for a school, but fundamentally, if people do not believe in you and have not bought into your vision and you as a person, then it is 'goodnight Vienna'.

As a very inexperienced senior leader, I was once told by a much wiser deputy head, 'Leadership and being a leader is no longer about you, Sam. It is no longer about you doing, doing and doing some more. It is no longer about how many tasks you can complete. It is about how you bring the best out in others.' I remember hearing this and thinking, in my professionally naïve state, this sounded like madness, coupled with some expletives. Surely leadership is about doing lots of things, being busy, being seen to be busy and being seen to be working hard. How wrong the younger version of me was. The deputy head mentoring me, once the penny had dropped, had gifted me with some of the most savvy professional advice I had ever been afforded. In short, the advice I was given was 'slow down, calm, stop being an adrenaline junky and think about others'. Wise words.

The first key people to consider are the members of the inner cabinet – the senior team. As a leader, especially the head, it is all too tempting to build a team of people who are carbon copies of yourself. There is something reassuring about constructing a senior team of people that mirror you; how you think, how you work, how you construct ideas and that, when crunch time comes, will say 'yes'. However, this is not always the wisest move. You do want people who are fundamentally mission aligned, who believe in you and the vision for the school, but if everyone is a 'yes' person, you will inevitably come into trouble. You need a team of leaders who complement one another, who are not frightened to challenge decisions (respectfully and behind closed doors), who can think for themselves, who can take the initiative, and who can make decisions and lead without having to seek permission for every breath that they take. Ideally you need what is called a jigsaw approach, where each individual within the team is different but they come together tightly as one.

In many regards, when you are considering the team that you want, it is worth thinking about Yin and Yang. Take the time to undertake a skills audit of your team and consider the strengths and areas for development of your team members. This, again, is why it is so important for leaders to know who they are. If they do, then this exercise becomes a lot easier and is more likely to be successful. You can then use this intelligence to think carefully about the type of people you need in your team to complement one another and potentially serve as the Yin and Yang to one another. Your ideal is a team who are cognitively diverse. The Harvard Business Review found that the wider the array of views in a team, the better the team's performance.[3]

---

3   https://hbr.org/2016/09/diverse-teams-feel-less-comfortable-and-thats-why-they-perform-better

Of course, the reality when you join a school or step up as a leader is that you will be inheriting and/or joining an established team. It will have its own established dynamic, routines and personalities. You will need to think carefully about how you will fit into this team or, indeed, lead it. It is crucial that you get to know the individuals that comprise the senior team of the school and understand what motivates them. A key action for any given head is to find out who your generals are. Who are the people who really buy into you and can carry the respect of the staff and community as a whole? These people are your cultural architects and will help to influence the mindsets of others. They can be identified by their status, attitude and talent. Charging these people to lead – and lead without suffocation – will empower them. They are likely to run over hot coals for you and feel truly valued. The chances are that their influence will have a snowball effect on other members of staff, and before you know it, they will have helped you to generate broader and wider buy-in for your vision and ethos. This is really powerful.

Within any given team, it is really important that you know how people work and what motivates them. You will have people who have low self-esteem, people who suffer from imposter syndrome, people who start initiatives but never see them through, people who like to talk a lot but do very little, people who are human dynamos, people who can read the room and those who are completely incapable of it, people who can speak publicly and those who run from the challenge and head for the hills. Some people will thrive off praise, some thrive (even if it seems counter-intuitive) off criticism, some people simply enjoy working hard, and some people have lower expectations than you might like. Deci and Ryan talk about autonomy, competence and relatedness. The diverse range of skill sets, expertise, knowledge and abilities across your staff can and will be huge.

A crucial element of leadership is developing buy-in and trust. Trust is a fundamental aspect of any successful working relationship. Your staff and your immediate team need to be able to trust you, to believe in you and to know that you will consistently support them as and when they need it. As Stephen M. R. Covey says in *The Speed of Trust*, 'Trust has the potential to create unparalleled success and prosperity in every dimension of life, but it is the least understood, most neglected and most underestimated possibility of our time.' The reality is that building trust requires hard work, effort and clear demonstrable acts. You can rebuild trust once it is lost, but this takes even greater effort. You must demonstrate that you trust your team/colleagues to do their jobs. If you do not afford others the professional trust to execute their responsibilities, then you will cause more harm than good. It is important to consider how much you could slow down decision making, progress and innovation if you do not trust your colleagues and if you seek, ultimately, to micromanage their every move. At the absolute worst, you could create resentment within your team. In seeking to build trust, I would urge you to consider the following:

1.  Do you lead with integrity and are you able to walk the walk and not just talk the talk? Actively doing things you expect others to do counts for a lot.

2.  Are you able to lead with clear intent and absolute transparency? The more you keep your cards to your chest, the less likely people are to trust you.

3.  Do you possess the relevant level of competency to execute your role or are you determined to show willing with areas you are perhaps less confident in?

4.  Whatever action you take, is there a clear outcome? Is there a clear result that you can refer to and staff can see?

5.  Do you actively listen to your colleagues and take on board their feedback and appraisal of situations?

6.  Do you extend trust to those you work with so they can demonstrate their competency?

In building trust, you are also trying to create a sense of identity. If you create a sense of identity, you will create a sense of belonging. When people feel, deeply and almost innately, that they belong to a school or an organisation, they become invested in the place that they work. People become far more loyal, committed and willing to go the extra mile. Your role as a leader is to instil in all of your stakeholders, especially the staff and children, that they belong to a special group, that there are high standards and expectations that underpin this group and, crucially, that you believe that they can match and exceed those expectations and achieve great things. You need to instil in people that you believe in them. If you can achieve this, then you will fundamentally shift people's mindsets. This is why carefully considering what your mission statement, vision and values are is essential to the success of any organisation. If people live and breathe what your school is about, they will work even harder for you than you could imagine.

Taking all of the points I have raised so far, it is really important that you take the time to carefully consider how you support your colleagues. As Lee Shulman said, 'Those who can, do. Those that understand, teach.'[4] If we truly, as leaders, want to build trust and a relationship with our staff then it is crucial that we consider the conditions they are operating in and allow them to do their jobs as effectively as possible. The magic within education happens in classrooms. Teaching is a complex art form. It is theatre. It is panto. It is drama. Even the most introverted of teachers has to adopt an extrovert persona as they take centre stage.

Every single day hundreds of thousands of teachers up and down the land are expected, lesson after lesson, to walk into a classroom and engage, teach and inspire a group of pupils (30 on average). In a primary setting, the teacher invariably has the same set of 30 children all day, every day. In a secondary school, any given teacher will encounter a new and different set of pupils every lesson. The physical demands alone of sustaining this over a six-, seven- or eight-week window are huge. Sandwiched between these lessons are often break duties, routine meetings and extracurricular clubs. After school, staff are often once again involved in meetings and then have the small matter of marking, planning, responding to emails and other associated administrative tasks that 'need' to be performed, as well as carefully considering their subject knowledge, their use of questioning and pre-empting misconceptions that pupils may have. This is no small ask.

Workload remains a significant issue for teachers. Many teachers will work 60+ hours a week. By week five of any given half-term, it will feel like you have hit the wall. To sustain doing all of the associated tasks attached to the role, let alone the actual classroom delivery, will require even the most superhuman of teachers to dig deep, again and again.

---

4    Shulman, L. (1986) 'Those who understand: Knowledge growth in teaching.' *Educational Researcher*, 15(2): pp. 4–14.

So, what can be done? If we take out the obvious big and significant wins – money, pay, recruitment, more teachers, increased PPA, remote working and flexible working – then we need to look at what else is within the sector's gift.

First and foremost is mindset. We need to adopt a positive mindset about teaching. I do not mean one that is delusional and shouting out 'but teaching is a calling'. This approach, which was employed several decades ago, no longer washes. We need to think carefully about what the actual purpose of a teacher is. Ironically, a bit like a Ronseal advert, the clue is in the name. As Sir John Jones says, teaching is a magic weaving business, and the 'magic' happens in the classroom. So, if we are insistent on teachers doing things outside of the classroom, we really need to consider:

- Why?
- To what end?
- Is it sensible, realistic and practical?
- Does it serve a purpose?
- What else needs to go to make room for this?
- What impact will X have on classroom delivery and the children that we serve?
- What are the unintended consequences?

These are key questions any leader worth their salt should be asking themselves. Views of 'we have always done it that way' or 'when I used to teach history...' are at best unhelpful. It is really important that time, care and consideration are taken to dissect any task that is set that transcends the classroom setting.

Key areas of focus for staff should include:

- The approach to meetings, including the volume, purpose and length.
- Duties – is it sensible for a staff member to conduct a duty during a five-period day? When do they get to eat, breathe, have a drink or go to the toilet?
- Extracurricular activities – are staff forced to take part?

- Lunch breaks – are staff directed to work during lunch?
- The approach to marking – is this sensible, sustainable and does it have impact?
- The approach to behaviour – how supportive, clear and sensible are the approaches? Can staff ultimately teach disruption free?
- The approach to emails – different people have different views on this item, but there is a huge danger that we are becoming a 24/7 industry.
- The timing of school improvement – are staff given the time, training and ability to think through your changes at a whole-school level?
- The allocation and use of PPA – can staff take this time off-site and use it as they wish?
- Cover – are we adhering to the principles of rarely cover?
- Mocksteds – do we need these? What impact do they have on the school community?
- Homework – what is the expectation here and is there any associated marking?
- Co-planning – some people are resistant to this, but why do we need to reinvent the same wheel over and over and over?

These are just a few of the things that can be done to support teachers. Crucially, they are considerations to support their work–life balance. It is really important that we remember teaching is a marathon, not a sprint. One thing we should never forget though, is to say 'thank you' to a teacher. Praise, care and kindness from pupils and leaders alike goes a long, long way.[5]

If we are to effect change as leaders, then there are four important considerations to ponder over. Firstly, who are your early adopters? This is the Apple approach but equally applicable to education. If you want to launch a big change in your school, why not undertake a try-before-you-buy position? Ask a few people who you know will run with an idea,

---

5    I originally wrote this section for the Edpsy blog, which can be found here: https://edpsy.org.uk/blog/2023/phronesis-the-wisdom-of-workload-on-world-teachers-day/

change or approach and then, once they have actioned it, ask them for their honest feedback regarding its efficacy. These people are likely to spread the word and support your proposed change if the initial trial has been a success. However, if your early adopters respond that approach X does not work, then you need to be able to listen to and heed the warning.

Secondly, give people time. Consider carefully that as a leader you are likely to have spent some considerable time researching a change. You may have read multiple books, articles and research papers. You may have visited other schools to see an approach in action. You may even have spent considerable time with other leaders discussing a proposed change. Do not, therefore, think that by announcing a change on a Friday, it can come into play on a Monday. This does not give staff the time or space to consider what you want, how to actually do it or to be properly trained. If you act in this rushed manner with staff, you will lose their confidence and trust and, in turn, they will lose personal confidence in their own ability to do their job too. Keep things, as best you can, simple and low stakes, and try to build an autotelic experience for your colleagues. In other words, make things flow.

Thirdly, be wary, as Toto Wolff warns, of people who say, 'We have always done it this way.' Sometimes this can be a positive, but sometimes this is a real negative. Finally, communicate in person as much as possible. As actor Bob Hoskins said, 'It is good to talk.' Be it other leaders, governors, central team members, staff, pupils, parents, etc., the more you can communicate in person and in a personable manner, the better.

To bring this chapter to a close, I think it is important that you consider seven key questions when seeking to action anything, as follows:

1. Why are you doing this?
2. What are you looking to do?
3. When will you launch it?
4. Which strategy or approach will you take?
5. Who will action it?
6. What are the possible unintended consequences of your change?
7. What do you want the impact to be?

As Glinda the Good Witch from *The Wizard of Oz* once said, 'You've always had the power my dear, you just had to learn it for yourself.'

Now would be a good time to write down five key takeaways that you will action for yourself on the basis of what you have read in chapter four.

**Considerations:**

**1**
_____

_____

_____

**2**
_____

_____

_____

**3**
_____

_____

_____

**4**
_____

_____

_____

**5**
_____

_____

_____

# CHAPTER 5:
# BEHAVIOUR –
# THE LEADERSHIP HILL

> This chapter will focus on two important elements:
> 1. The importance of leading on behaviour
> 2. Considerations to ensure you get behaviour right.

As a young boy I was, generally speaking, well behaved. I did as I was told, and I helped my mum to keep our house clean and tidy. Every now and then, however, I would do something silly that would grate with my dad. My dad, in true parental fashion, would reprimand me by raising his voice and telling me, 'You just need to behave,' often followed by, 'Go to your room and have a think about how you are behaving.' At that point I would go to my room, often upset, but ultimately not really knowing what I needed to do in order to behave. If we flip this into the school universe, how often do we see staff say to children 'you just need to behave' or 'you need to learn to behave' with a raised and stern voice? In a school setting, just like with the younger version of me, this mystical strapline is meaningless. It does not magically lead to children behaving. Why? Because ultimately this is a game of 'guess what is in my head'. As the parent – or in a school setting, the teacher – uttering this phrase is meaningless. Unless you have explained, modelled and taught precisely what good behaviour actually looks like, children do not know. They cannot magically visualise what positive behaviour is. Most children actually want to impress adults.

Most children do not enjoy getting into trouble. It is our job to support children to make the right behavioural choices and show them how to do it, otherwise they will not succeed. It is also worth considering that most children do not aspire to fail. Most children do not want to stuff up their exams, go on to earn very little money or live on the streets and beg for money and food. Therefore, the culture of aspiration and ambition that we set children up with is crucial.

In the same way that we need to be explicit with children about what we want from them in terms of behaviour, we also need to adopt the same approach and mindset with the staff we lead. Imagine for a moment that I gave an entire staffing body a one wood golf club and said to them all, 'I want you to hit 10 balls in a straight line, off you go.' Some people may be able to do this perfectly as they are naturally good at golf, some may well struggle but will hit the ball with varying degrees of success, some may struggle to hit the ball at all and some may not even be able to hold the club properly. If we extrapolate this analogy to behaviour, the point remains true. There are some staff who, through force of personality, can 'do behaviour', and there are some staff who struggle with it. This is where the narrative that 'behaviour is all about relationships' is lazy at best and fundamentally fails teachers at worst. How, for example, does the teacher in a secondary school who sees a Year 9 class once a fortnight build relationships with the pupils? This is hugely challenging. My point here is that without clear, explicit and repeated training and support for staff, they will ultimately struggle. Telling staff 'I want you to teach really effective disruption-free lessons' without training them in how to do it is the same as telling Sam aged 8 'you just need to behave'. In short, it is a pointless waste of breath and a waste of everyone's finite time. So, my starting point with behaviour and leadership is that leaders, especially the head, need to be explicitly clear with what they want for behaviour, in terms of both positive and negative behaviours. If this is not a clear leadership priority, irrespective of how good a school may or may not be, then leaders will (as referenced in the previous chapter) lose the faith and trust of the staff and pupils. It is therefore essential that leaders make it easy for staff to be consistent. If leaders fail to do this, then they are not sufficiently supporting their staff.

Whether we like it or not, behaviour will make or break how a leadership team and a school are viewed by an entire community. Behaviour in all of its facets will define your school's culture. Positive behaviour will allow pupils to achieve more academically and serve to reverse the Matthew Effect, where disadvantaged pupils are behind their more fortunate peers and become more disadvantaged over time. A strong approach to behaviour will allow teachers to reclaim the most finite entity that they have: time. It will allow them to teach effectively and efficiently. This, in turn, will lead to improved staff satisfaction and wellbeing, and will invariably bolster both recruitment and retention, as teachers will talk amongst their peers and tell each other which schools are/are not worth working at. By the same token, parents talk, and they know which schools take behaviour seriously. If you want to see your number on roll reduce at speed, then let behaviour slide. A culture of positive behaviour will serve as one of your strongest marketing tools. Devolve behaviour to someone else and you are, like arming staff with a one wood golf club, leaving your school improvement journey to chance and the variable abilities across your staff. Behaviour fundamentally defines everything. If you don't believe me, then please consider the following two quotes:

1. 'Creating a culture with high expectations of behaviour will benefit both teachers and pupils, establishing calm, orderly, safe and supportive environments conducive to learning.' The Department for Education, 2024[6]

2. 'Good discipline in schools is essential to ensure that all pupils can benefit from the opportunities provided by education.' The Department for Education, 2013[7]

People talk of a behaviour curriculum. I hear people citing the need to deliver it as part of a 20-minute tutor time once a week and that there needs to be a document or a scheme of work for it. In my view, this is not what a behaviour curriculum is. A behaviour curriculum is something that is lived and breathed by everyone in your school and is seamlessly interwoven into every aspect of your overall curriculum, culture and

---

6    https://assets.publishing.service.gov.uk/media/65ce3721e1bdec001a3221fe/Behaviour_in_schools_-_advice_for_headteachers_and_school_staff_Feb_2024.pdf

7    https://explore-education-statistics.service.gov.uk/methodology/pupil-exclusion-statistics-methodology

ethos. If it becomes a bolt-on 'behaviour curriculum' session it simply will not work. It needs to be part of the constant narration of expectations, manners and values in your school.

Like it or not, behaviour is the foundation upon which all of your school improvement will be and should be built. This starts with the head and their approach to behaviour. Their values, their philosophy and what they hold dear. This then extends to the senior leadership team and leaders all across the school, then to teaching staff and then to all other staff that work in the school. Behaviour is more than simply rules. It is every interaction, every element of modelling, narration and scaffolding of the school's core values, ethos and vision. I have emphasised earlier on in this book the importance of your school's mission statement, vision and values. These core components will, if lived and breathed properly, define the culture of your school and behaviour. And whilst you may well know what your rules, mission statement, vision, values and ethos are, it is important to consider, question and ascertain whether the staff and pupils do too. This is the acid test to ascertain whether what your school is about is truly part of the overall daily narrative or not.

As a leader, it is worth considering just how important behaviour is, especially to staff. Over a quarter of teachers (sometimes more depending on the poll) think that behaviour is not good enough. Polls undertaken by students show that over half of the students canvassed do not believe behaviour is good enough. Yet leaders, when polled, do not share these same thoughts. They do not seem, generally speaking, to think it is as bad as students and teachers suggest. There is a real disconnect here. It is worth considering carefully why staff and pupils can and do feel this way. Critically, have you given careful consideration to the programme of professional development and support for your staff, and have you built systems and processes that are proactive as opposed to reactive in nature and design? These are important points to ponder on.

It is really important that you do not fall into the trap of believing that good lesson planning automatically leads to good lessons. Whilst no one would dispute that good planning helps, it is meaningless if poor behaviour is the established norm in your school. You need to build a policy, approach and set of systems that ultimately, however you strip it, allow teachers to teach disruption free. More importantly, you need to build a culture that allows the most novice and least confident member of your teaching body to be able to teach and flourish.

When considering your whole-school approach, time needs to be taken to consider the following key elements that make up your behavioural approach:

- What do you define positive and negative behaviour as?

- What are your rules?

- What are your lines in the sand? In other words, what are the behaviours you simply will not allow?

- What is your view on suspensions and exclusions?

- What is your view on detentions? If you do have them, how will they work?

- What is your view on isolation? If you adopt this approach, how will this function?

- How are classrooms laid out? Does classroom design allow teachers to teach and serve as the experts in the room, or are they vying for the attention of the pupils because the classroom layouts do not support the style of learning that they are engaging the pupils with?

- What is your educational philosophy and how do you want your pupils in your school to be taught?

- How do you want pupils to enter the school at the start of the day and leave the school at the end of the day?

- How do you want pupils to transition through the day if they are moving classrooms/teachers? How do you want pupils to behave in the corridors of the school?

- How do you want pupils to enter assembly?

- How do you want break and lunch to look and be supervised?

- What are your views on lesson punctuality?

- What are your views on toilet usage?

- Do you want an on-call system with duty rota staff to support teachers through the day?

- What are your views on rewards? How will this look?

- Do you want a year team system? Or do you want a house system? Or do you want both or a hybrid or something else?

- How will you engage parents?

- What are your views on uniform?

- What are your views on pupils equipping themselves so they are ready to learn versus the school providing the pupils with everything that they need?

- How many warnings will children be given before they are issued with a sanction?

- What is your view on restorative justice as an approach?

- How do you want your pupils to interact with visitors?

- How will you support pupils with genuine needs (e.g. SEN, unmet needs, trauma or safeguarding-induced needs)?

- How do you want safeguarding to work? What is the safeguarding culture that you want to see in your school?

- How will you tackle truancy?

- What is your view on character?

- What is your view on manners?

- How will your approach to behaviour endorse your values?

These are but some of the crucial questions you need to ask yourself when you are considering behaviour as a leader. As a leadership team, you need to know the answers here. You need to have a plan and a strategy for each and every one of these questions and no doubt more. Once you know what you want, and without wishing to repeat myself, you need to train everyone in your school – pupils and staff alike – so that what you want is known, understood and sticks. Try to consider the following approach:

As a general rule of thumb, the most successful schools tend to share five common traits: they have highly visible leaders; there is clarity over the culture; the culture is underpinned by sky-high expectations; there are high levels of support for both staff and pupils alike; and they are really, really, really consistent. Consistency is key to behaviour because everyone knows where they stand. Consistency brings about certainty and children thrive in environments that are safe, secure, certain and supportive but also underpinned with professional warmth and love.

You should have really simple and clear approaches that people can easily understand and action. I would create a really simple aide-memoire for your staff so they know what to do day in, day out. The following is a simple illustration of some really clear routinised expectations that could form a teaching code of conduct for your staff:

- Be on time and have all your resources prepared.
- Meet and greet the pupils with a warm welcome.
- Have a clear starter activity for pupils to undertake.
- Take the register.
- Engage in a question and answer session following your starter activity.
- Share the aim of the lesson with the pupils.
- Explicitly teach your lesson routines to your pupils.
- Use praise appropriately.
- Give lots of verbal feedback in real time.
- Follow the behaviour policy with consistency.
- Have a clear exit routine.
- Script key behaviour approaches you are not confident with until they become habitual.

I will close this chapter with one crucial piece of advice regarding behaviour: all leaders should have behaviour as part of their job description. Behaviour needs to be a collective team effort and not left solely to one leader to fight their way through on their own.

Now would be a good time to write down five key takeaways that you will action for yourself on the basis of what you have read in chapter five.

**Considerations:**

**1**
_____

_____

_____

**2**
_____

_____

_____

**3**
_____

_____

_____

**4**
_____

_____

_____

**5**
_____

_____

_____

## CHAPTER 6:

# LEADING ON THE CURRICULUM – AN AGENCY FOR GOOD

This chapter will focus on two important elements:

1.  The importance of leading on curriculum
2.  Considerations to ensure you get the curriculum right.

A lot has been said about curriculum in recent years, and whilst I have really appreciated the influx of ideas, thoughts and considerations on this topic, I will also say this: curriculum has become a far more complex beast than it actually needs to be. Complex ideas and language are used a lot when discussing curriculum. It has been taken almost beyond PhD-level thinking and, arguably, one key stakeholder has been forgotten in the process – the children! The more complex, the more difficult and the more clever we try to be with the curriculum, the more likely we are to lose children. Leaders absolutely must own the curriculum. I have deliberately put behaviour before curriculum in this book because if behaviour is not right then everything falls apart. But curriculum is your next big driver in changing your school. The curriculum, underpinned by good behaviour, will serve as the heartbeat of your school and can serve as an agent for social justice. Leaders have to know what the curriculum in their school stands for, what it is about and how it intermeshes and embodies the school's values.

As a starting point, leaders should carefully consider what they want the children in their school to be able to do by the time they leave each key stage and leave the school entirely. This could be a set of knowledge bases, a series of core skills (based, I would argue, in disciplinary knowledge) or a set of character values. My point here is that you need to know what your end goal is. This should be underpinned by your school's values and ethos, which again provide your 'why' for all that you do. Some schools talk about having a 'way' (for example, this is 'the Hogwart Academy way'). Whilst this may sound clichéd, it is actually a really useful exercise for leaders to engage in as it focuses both hearts and minds to nail your colours to the mast and clearly label what your school is about. This should serve as your starting point.

Consideration then needs to be given to the composition of the curriculum. This is the nuts-and-bolts aspect, often dubbed by some as boring and 'not what curriculum is'. However, if you have not given consideration to the following, you are in trouble:

- What subjects will you offer? Free schools and academies have far more freedom and scope than local authority schools.

- How much freedom do you want to afford to staff to pick what they teach?

- Does your curriculum adhere to the national curriculum?

- How many hours per week will you give each subject? This can have a huge impact on academic outcomes and will hugely influence staffing models.

- Will you push the EBacc? Will you promote the arts? Will you push PE?

- How long will you spend on KS3 and KS4?

- How many periods a week will you assign to KS5 lessons?

- Where does oracy sit within your curriculum?

- Will you operate a one-week or two-week timetable? This applies more to secondary. If you are adopting a two-week timetable, how frequently and consistently will pupils come into contact with their teachers? Consider the member of staff who sees their groups once per fortnight: what does this mean for their subject, for their ability to teach effectively and for knowledge retention? On the flip side, if you have a one-week timetable, does this allow for enough curricular flexibility?

- Will you set your classes? Or will you adopt a mixed attainment approach? Or will you adopt a hybrid model with mixed sets and a top set, etc.?

- Where will you ensure children have access to the teaching of careers, PSHE and RSE?

- What support and interventions are in place for children who are not secondary ready or falling behind in phonics, reading, writing and numeracy?

- What emphasis will you place on reading?

- What is your approach to children with SEND?

- How will your curriculum promote character and your school values?

- How will you ensure that children learn and retain more knowledge over time?

- How do you celebrate pupil work within the curriculum?

- How does behaviour explicitly interlink with the curriculum and ultimately become a part of the curriculum, rather than serving as a bolt-on?

- Will you control the mode of delivery across the school so that staff have to use workbooks, visualisers, mini-whiteboards, textbooks, exercise books, etc.?

- What do you take a broad and balanced curriculum to be?

- What will be the balance between knowledge and disciplinary skills?

- How will you quality assure your curriculum so you, as leaders, know it is effective?

- How will you ensure that the curriculum upholds the values that you have created for the school and has a positive impact?

- How will you support staff to get even better at delivering the curriculum?

All of these questions around the curriculum are crucial. Leaders need to know the answers to these and clearly nail their colours to the mast. Again, like behaviour, this should not be left simply to one member of staff. This should be the responsibility of an entire leadership team. In all cases, the answers and the direct application of the answers to the questions I have posed will serve to define your school's ethos and what people see on a day-to-day basis. Once you know the answers to these questions, you can then give some thought to your staffing model. Very much like the Boyatzis model that I referred to earlier on in this book, you will have a staffing model that you have inherited as a leader/leadership team. But you need to consider what your ideal staffing body will look like, the positions you need filling and the type of people you want to see working in your school. For example, if you want to promote the EBacc but only have two languages teachers and you want 80% of the cohort to take a language at GCSE, it is highly likely that in your ideal universe you are going to have to at least double the size of the department. These are all critical considerations for leaders.

You then need to consider subject leadership. To what extent have you trained staff, both middle leaders and teaching staff, in the dark arts of curricular design and curriculum theory? This is professional knowledge that they need to know and master. This is where your approach to meetings and schedules needs careful thought. There are two elements to curriculum here. One is school-wide curricular training. The other is subject-specific curricular training. For leaders, the latter point is a challenge because, as with all things in leadership, you only know what you know. You need to ensure that you have invested in your subject leaders with quality, external, subject-specific training if you do not possess the necessary in-house expertise. Your subject leaders need to know their onions and, in turn, be able to train up their teams in subject-specific matters.

Subject leaders need to take the time to really consider their curriculum and home in on the following:

- What should pupils be able to do once they have finished studying a subject?
- For any given key stage, what do subject leaders want a pupil to be able to do and to have learnt in their subject?

- For any given topic, what do subject leaders want a pupil to be able to do and to have learnt in their subject?

I would promote subject leaders to create a subject intent statement. This has nothing to do with satisfying Ofsted, which is a futile pursuit. This is about subject leaders and their teams sitting down and thinking hard about their subject's importance and place within the wider curriculum. If staff do not know what their subject is about, why pupils should study it and what they want the pupils to walk away with, then who does? How do they justify their subject's curricular positioning to themselves, let alone the pupils? Avoiding this does staff a huge disservice. Time needs to be devoted to formulating the curricular tools that will allow this curricular intent to become a living, breathing and taught reality. I strongly advocate creating schemes of work and co-planned resources in subject communities. Without these in place (and I appreciate that if a team is starting from scratch, it is a labour of love to create them), the curriculum almost becomes something that is made up as you go along, and staff invariably fall into the trap of an activity-led curriculum. Ideally you want staff to be in a position where they can consider their subject knowledge, their approaches to questioning, how they model and break down problems, and how they pre-empt misconceptions with pupils. These are the curricular enactment tools that make the biggest difference. Once this is in place, subject leaders can then carefully consider the following core questions about their subject-based curriculum:

- Does the curriculum demonstrate that there is high ambition for all students?

- Is the curriculum broad and balanced? In particular, do all students have full access to the national curriculum programmes of study in all subjects?

- Are any adaptations made to the curriculum for SEND and the most disadvantaged students?

- Have the subject leaders assured and ensured appropriate and logical content choices and sequencing? Does curriculum planning help students to remember and know more over time?

- To what extent is there an all-through curriculum intent across subjects?

- To what extent is assessment in all its forms effective?

It is also worth considering, as Philip Jackson, professor and author, stated in 1968, that what is taught in schools is more than the sum total of the curriculum. Jackson thought that schooling should be understood as a socialisation process where pupils pick up messages through the experiences of being in school, not just from the things that they are explicitly taught. I would take this a step further and argue that the knowledge pupils have learnt and are able to apply is also a product of the acquired knowledge effect – in other words, the social and cultural capital that they have been exposed to by their respective families. Some children possess more of this than others and it is why, as previously raised in this book, context is key. Not all contexts are the same and some children or cohorts/communities of children are at a far greater advantage than others. As a leader you need to know this, as this will influence your curricular decision making.

My final thought, as I draw this chapter to a close, is that the curriculum is a process. It is not an event. And, like any process, it never truly comes to an end. Equally, all processes involve change and this involves people. If you want to have a successful curriculum then, in truth, you are only going to be as successful as the sum of your parts and the investment, time and training that you put into people. This is why your most valuable resource in any given school is the staff. This is why whatever school improvement decisions you make as a leader must always, always, always come back to what impact will they have on the staff and therefore the pupils. As I laboured in *Education Exposed 2* and earlier on in this book, the magic in education happens in the classrooms of our schools. Let staff pursue the halcyon dream, namely inspiring children to learn through well-taught lessons.

Now would be a good time to write down five key takeaways that you will action for yourself on the basis of what you have read in chapter six.

**Considerations:**

**1**

**2**

**3**

**4**

**5**

CHAPTER 7:
# CULTURE IS KING

This chapter will focus on two important elements:
1. Who actually drives culture
2. The importance of culture.

A lot is made of culture. Who drives it, where it comes from, whether it is some sort of invisible entity, whether it is amorphous... The list goes on. My view is that culture is anything but amorphous. It is not some sort of abstract ideal. I am yet to work in a school where if a headteacher says 'no' to an initiative or idea, it subsequently happens. The head, as per the headteacher standards, should set the school's culture, unless of course the head is a vanguard, in which case the head is a defender of the established norm. All leaders have a duty and moral responsibility to support and defend the culture that the head sets.

Within this comes the debate about what makes a great teacher and what makes a great leader. Some say that great teachers do not always make great leaders, and others say you do not have to be a great teacher to be a great leader. My view is that we need great teachers, and we need lots of them. We want as many great teachers to flood our classrooms and inspire the children in our schools as humanly possible. However, if you are to lead teachers, you need to have earned your stripes. If you want to lead on teaching and learning, then I firmly believe you have to put your money where your mouth is. If you want to lead on behaviour, then you have to know your onions. I would not want a team of leaders to be made up of people who are not particularly effective at their craft. I do not know how you can carry the respect of staff otherwise. By the same token, the head, in my view, has to have worn multiple hats and have performed a variety of core tasks effectively in their career. If, sat in the chair, you do not know the complexities of the timetable, how behaviour works, how curriculum works, how to teach, and teach really well, then you will be quickly found wanting. Some will argue that you can farm things off to others, who are experts. Of course, this is true. You can. But how do you truly know what you, as a leader, want? How do you know if what you are being told is actually right? There are, naturally, best bet solutions, but fundamentally you may not be 100% certain of an approach if you have never done it yourself. There is a real danger in leadership that the Dunning-Kruger effect can creep in (where a person overestimates their abilities as a result of a lack of knowledge about a particular situation). In line with the theme of this book, school improvement should not be a race and neither should your career progression. Double or triple jumping critical core positions in a bid to race to the top runs the risk of leaving you in a precarious position as a leader and is potentially unfair on the community you seek to support.

Culture, rightly, is a building block of school improvement. It cannot be detached from a school's mission statement, ethos, vision, values, behavioural approaches, curriculum, approaches to staffing, teaching and learning, etc. because culture underpins all of these things. By the same token, all of these drivers are part and parcel of a school's culture. Culture is a fundamental cornerstone of the headteacher standards and with good reason. Therefore, culture is a manifestation of the head's values, morals, ethos and educational beliefs. Leaders should embody this culture and defend it (as stated in previous chapters). A few questions to ponder on when considering your culture are:

- What is it like to work and teach in your school, all day, every day?
- How often do you focus on and celebrate the positives within your school with your community?
- To what extent do you create a sense of belonging?
- Do you support teaching and learning so that feedback both enables and empowers staff to positively drive the curriculum?

Anyone visiting a school should be able to both feel and identify a school's culture from the moment they drive into the school grounds. This culture should then manifest itself in the shared beliefs, routines, norms and traditions that are visible across the school. The overall level of expectations and how people – all people – behave is another important representation of the culture generated in a school. The artefacts across the school serve as a visual representation to reinforce the culture. It is important to consider the following questions:

1. What do you want the culture of your school to say about the type of school that you are?

2. What do you want people to think your school stands for?

3. How will you ensure that your culture is lived and breathed?

The last question is critical. Whilst arguably you can flip a school on its head quite swiftly, and for the better, it takes time to develop, teach and embed the culture that you want.

Culture drives so many elements of school life. A positive culture will support learning, wellbeing, workload, positive behaviour, character and attendance. Crucially, it has a huge impact on pupil attainment. Whilst we can argue that school life is more than a set of academic outcomes, we also need to be realistic – a strong set of GCSEs and post-16 outcomes serve as an invaluable set of keys that open up the doors of opportunity for our children, and without these keys their chances of succeeding in their aspirations and ambitions are restricted and more difficult. It also goes without saying that schools where pupils consistently achieve strong outcomes across multiple subjects invariably have teachers who consistently adhere to and uphold the culture of the school. So, a challenge for leaders is to consider how clear, purposeful and easy to understand the culture of their school is. In short, do people get it? A positive culture should allow teachers to teach, ideally disruption free. It should allow pupils to learn and for the social norm to positively shift. Crucially, though, it should inspire everyone to be proud of the school and demonstrate great pride that they work for and/or attend your school.

The other reality of a positive school culture (just like a negative one) is that it is infectious. It accumulates. You are able to build on it, year on year, and assuming you maintain an upward trajectory of positivity, you will find that your school gets better and better and better. This is where the restless school analogy, courtesy of Roy Blatchford, really comes into its own.[8] As you build your school and both behaviour and the curriculum are able to take their grip, you can then look to really sharpen your school improvement saw. It is equally as important as a leader that you know when to say no. What actually needs doing, what is twaddle and what serves as a major distraction from your goals? I would recommend taking some time to consider the working week ahead and write down 10 things you know you have to do. Then consider carefully whether those 10 things help you to achieve your goals and/or actually need doing. Are they actually relevant? If not, ignore them. This is challenging for us all because as teachers we do not like to say no and often feel hugely guilty when we do.

To conclude this chapter, as Dylan Wiliam says, 'If we create a culture where everyone believes they need to improve, not because they are not good enough, but because they can be even better, there is no limit to what we can achieve.'[9] In order to do this, considering all of the points I have raised in this book, the key thing you need to do is lead with care.

Now would be a good time to write down five key takeaways that you will action for yourself on the basis of what you have read in chapter seven.

---

8    www.amazon.co.uk/Restless-School-Roy-Blatchford/dp/190971707X
9    Quoted in: *The Innovator's Mindset: Empower Learning, Unleash Talent, and Lead a Culture of Creativity* by George Couros.

**Considerations:**

**1**

_____

_____

_____

**2**

_____

_____

_____

**3**

_____

_____

_____

**4**

_____

_____

_____

**5**

_____

_____

_____

# CONCLUDING THOUGHTS

As I draw this book to a close, it is fair to say that leaders and leadership play an integral part in the success and improvement of any given school. By and large, student academic outcomes rarely outstrip the overall strength, capacity and potential of leadership, be it middle or – crucially – senior leadership within a school. It is therefore critical that leaders keep the focus on teaching. Leaders make a fundamental difference to the culture, climate and ethos of their schools. They are key to developing people and nurturing talent. Leaders should drive behaviour and ensure that teachers are able to thrive. Leaders therefore have a professional and moral responsibility to manage the wellbeing and workload of their staff. The simplest way I think about this is through martial arts and the teachings of Bruce Lee (of whom I am an avid fan). Bruce Lee talked extensively about taking the shortest route to execute an action. What is the quickest and simplest route to move or strike from point A to point B? Bringing this thinking into a school setting, how do we take staff from point A to point B without losing them? How do we keep things simple but effective? I believe the focus should be simple and kept to:

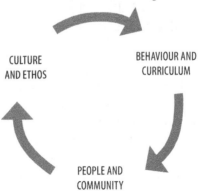

CULTURE AND ETHOS

BEHAVIOUR AND CURRICULUM

PEOPLE AND COMMUNITY

I have deliberately focused this book on seven core areas (you, leadership, your contextual setting, the people you work with, behaviour, curriculum and culture) because these are the things that make the biggest difference to a school and its trajectory of travel. You need to be comfortable in your own skin and know who you are, what makes you tick, what you are good at and what you need support with. You need to understand what the role and responsibilities of being a leader are and why you are conducting your role in the manner that you do. You need to firmly understand your context and the people that work within it. I would strongly argue that you then need to prioritise behaviour before thinking about curricular change to ultimately craft the culture that you want to see. Much beyond these seven core pillars, which I have dubbed the Strickland Leadership Code, is either gloss, red herrings or foci that will suck your time for little to no impact. The Strickland Leadership Code can be summarised as:

- Know who you are
- Understand what leadership means and what it is
- Know and respect your context
- Know, respect and support your people
- Positively drive behaviour
- Focus on the curriculum
- Build your culture.

Leaders make a huge difference. They shape a school's culture and climate. They develop people and spot talent. They should ensure that behaviour is positive and allows staff to teach disruption free. They actively monitor and try to improve workload so staff can pursue the halcyon dream – teaching.

There are two states in leadership once you have actioned the majority of your core changes. Both states bring dangers with them. The first state is where everything becomes metronomically boring. As a leader you have established your systems, your routines and your play script. Bar sharpening your approach with each passing year to make it better and better, the reality is you are not going to fundamentally change what you are doing. The old adage of 'if it ain't broke, don't fix it' comes to mind. The issue here is that the same habitual routines and systems have the potential to become stale and boring because you are doing the same thing, in the same way, every day. What you must keep in mind is that the certainty of your consistency invariably allows others the security to execute their jobs effectively. The danger when you are in this state is that you can let things slide because things are so good.

The second state is one of positive dissatisfaction. This where you are content, bordering on happy, with what you have achieved. But you still want to improve and are not totally satisfied with where you are. In this state we dare to take further chances and strive for better. In many regards this marries up with Roy Blatchford's work on the restless school. Arguably, this is a healthy phase to be in. But the warning is that you must ensure the balance between being content and striving for further change is sensible and realistic. Whilst you do not want your school to go stale, you also do not want to totally upset the apple cart and undermine everything.

I wanted to finish this book with 20 core pieces of advice, all of which you can take or leave:

1. Leadership is about creating a culture where teachers can flourish and teach disruption free.

2. Leadership is not a race; slow change is lasting change.

3. Poor behaviour is kryptonite to all that we seek to do.

4. You should clearly define and narrate the culture you want – if you do not know, no one will know.

5. Leaders set the standard.

6. Behaviour should be explicitly taught through all that we do and not seen as a bolt-on.

7. The behaviour system should support staff, empower them and leave them feeling confident.

8. Careful consideration should be given to the routines you want in your school.

9. You must know your pupils and their key cultural, educational and social touchstones.

10. Pupils need to have knowledge and know how to apply it.

11. Be clear on what you want pupils to know and what your curriculum stands for and says about your school.

12. Avoid the pitfall of staff planning an activity-driven curriculum.

13. The curriculum should serve as a progression model.

14. Teachers should be viewed as experts.

15. Professional development should allow staff to focus on their curriculum design, subject knowledge and lesson delivery.

16. Leaders need to tackle and reduce workload as much as possible.

17. Leaders should be highly visible and supportive.

18. Pay homage to your contextual setting but also maintain an open mind about changes that could and should be made in your school.

19. All leaders should have responsibility for behaviour and the curriculum; these are fundamental school improvement drivers.

20. A state of positive dissatisfaction and metronomic boredom is healthy, but do not allow yourself to become complacent and do not create change for change's sake.

A task worth conducting as a leadership team is the creation of a leadership pledge. Personally, I would consider using your school's core values as a bedrock for your pledge. Ideally you would have three or five core values. For each value consider two or three clear commitments you will make as leaders. This then becomes a pledge to share with your staff and, if you wish, your pupils. The pledge should serve as a clear commitment and standard that you will hold yourselves to and be accountable for. A good starting point – when considering the commitments you will make and uphold – is the headteacher standards.

To conclude, leadership is not a race. Sometimes taking our time is best. There is a need to bring people along with you because if the people you work with do not understand and do not truly know what you want then they are guessing. This could bring about confusion and discontent. When you think about leadership and school improvement, think tortoise and not hare. Going at pace is not always best and can unintentionally undermine you.

My final thought for you comes courtesy of the Fairy Godmother from *Cinderella*: 'Even miracles take a little time.'

Best of luck.

# NOTES

# NOTES

# NOTES

## THEY DON'T BEHAVE FOR ME: 50 CLASSROOM BEHAVIOUR SCENARIOS TO SUPPORT SECONDARY PHASE TEACHERS

ISBN: 9781398388666

*They Don't Behave for Me* supports teachers with some key behavioural scenarios – ranging from classroom disruption and rudeness, to bullying, fights, and even a lack of overall behavioural strategy at a school level. Sam Strickland draws on his own experience to illustrate 50 common situations that he has had to resolve, seek support with, or offer advice on, and which most teachers will face at some point as they progress through their career into middle and senior leadership. Each scenario is broken down into an outline of the issue, a what to do in the immediate now, and a follow-up set of next steps.

We should never condone poor behaviour – but how do we keep going and find the answers to resolve things when they go wrong? This book will guide you from some of the key challenges regularly faced by teachers towards your own approach to effective behavioural management.

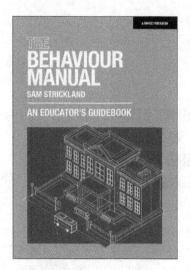

## THE BEHAVIOUR MANUAL: AN EDUCATOR'S GUIDEBOOK

ISBN: 9781915261243

*The Behaviour Manual: An Educator's Guidebook* offers over 100 strategies, approaches and teaching methods that will help any school, leader, middle leader, teacher, ECT or ITT to proactively lead on behaviour. It has been designed to help the entire profession and anyone at any level and all ranges of experience.

The book is divided into three broad sections. Section one examines the role of the mothership (the school) and the role that leaders at any level can play.

Section two looks at the role of the satellites (the key areas that make up the school) and the integral role that middle leaders play. The final section looks at the micro level, focusing on the role that teachers play, and offers a plethora of approaches teachers can employ.

Each of the 100+ strategies is unpacked over a spread. Within each spread is an outline of what the approach is. It is then unpacked to detail how it works or can be applied, and each spread finishes with a cautionary warning and an advice tip. This book is deliberately written to help, to offer support, to offer advice and there is, bluntly, no waffle, no padding and no fluff.

If you want a book that you can pick up, easily read and digest a key approach or strategy in less than 5–10 minutes, then this is for you. It is grounded in expertise, experience and research, and is deliberately written in a clear, straightforward and open style that leaves you in no doubt regarding how any of the given approaches work and could be employed in your school setting.

### For more information visit
### WWW.JOHNCATTBOOKSHOP.COM